# How's your dissertation going?

*If learners read about other learners having experiences similar to their own, they will be able to understand themselves better and be able to learn more effectively. At least, they will be comforted to know they are not the only ones in the world who have their struggle.*

*Boud, D (1987:12)*

# How's your dissertation going?

*Students share
the rough reality of dissertation
and project work*

**Liz Hampson**

*Innovation in
Higher Education Series*

**Unit for Innovation
in Higher Education**
School of Independent Studies
Lancaster University
Lancaster LA1 4YN

*First published in 1994 by the Unit for Innovation in Higher Education, School of Independent Studies, Lancaster University, Lancaster LA1 4YN*

ISBN 0 901800 51 1

PRINTED ON
RECYCLED PAPER

*Cover design by Rowland & Hird, Lancaster
Printed in Great Britain by Markprint,
Preston, Lancashire*

# Contents

# About the Author

Back in 1991, during an interview with an Admissions Tutor, I was asked a daunting question about my aspirations for the future – what was I hoping to do *after* graduation? Feeling rather intimidated, as a mature student returning to study after many years away from formal education, I remember blurting out that one of my aims was to write a book – this is it.

After completing the first year of my studies at the University of Central Lancashire, I then transferred to Lancaster University, graduating this year with a BA Honours degree in Human Communication. For me, the key to success was negotiation of responsible freedom in learning (two-thirds of my assessed work was submitted as dissertations and projects) and the help and encouragement of friends and family, both in and out of academic life.

The next step is postgraduate research – to learn more about undergraduates and their dissertations.

# Acknowledgments

My sincere thanks to each of the 59 students who generously agreed to contribute their unique experiences of doing a dissertation. I thank them for their trust, even though many are unknown to me personally, and for their willingness to share with other students. Without their generosity this book could not have become a reality.

I also wish to thank Peter Knight and John Wakeford for their genuine support, enthusiastic commitment and support.

My thanks also to friends and family for their patience, encouragement and good humour, all of which enabled me to pursue the idea of this book – it has been prepared by researching 'on', 'with' and 'for' other students. Thank you for believing in us and our efforts to make studying for a degree worthwhile.

# Introduction

## About the book

**This book is a kind of 'rough guide' which invites you to share students' experiences of doing a dissertation. It has been written by students, for students.**

You will not find conventional academic wisdom of the kind offered by authors of study skills books. Their prescriptive advice tends to flow in one direction only, ie. from experienced tutors ('the experts') to inexperienced students ('the confused'). This book offers something quite different; it is a dialogue between students, an 'insider' approach reflecting rough reality. This undergraduate's comment illustrates clearly the difference between conventional advice and the rather more unusual approach you will find here.

> The problem with books on 'how to write a dissertation' is that it sounds so cut and dried, polished, A B C - whereas for me, everything seemed muddled.

The research study, from which this book emerged, was carried out when I was one of 'the confused'. My own apprehensions when trying to write a dissertation for the first time were resolved, not through the expert guidance of tutors, but by my peers; we helped each other through the problems (and we shared the good times when things went well). This book is based on the hunch that if sharing our experiences worked for us, then it might work for you too.

During the second year of my degree, I had opted to write two dissertations and, although I was enthusiastic at first, I soon realised it was a whole new ball game and I didn't know the rules. When I looked for help, I found study skills texts in various guises but nearly all were aimed at an elite of dissertation-writers working at PhD level. There didn't seem to be anything available to be of any real help to an apprehensive undergraduate writing a dissertation for the first time. So I turned to other students, bought them coffees and asked, 'How's your dissertation going?'

This is the book that I wished had been available when I needed some reassurance. As it wasn't there, I decided to produce it myself - by asking other students who were also muddling along to contribute to this book (see Notes on Contributors, page 72, for details). Hopefully you will be encouraged by these recent graduates.

> It was helpful to see other people are going through the same difficulties...I gained the most important thing - self-confidence.

> You are never on your own - there is always someone around to give you support. Use it - don't worry alone.

> A student told me I was capable of doing a dissertation even though I doubted it myself. This gave me the inspiration and encouragement to go ahead.

In case you are wondering if all the students in this book were the type that 'just love intensive academic study', you may be interested to know that nearly two thirds were doing a compulsory dissertation, ie no dissertation, no degree! Their responses show that they have much in common but there are also plenty of contrasts and surprises. For example:

I enjoyed researching my dissertation more than anything else I did at University.

For me, the greatest pleasure came from finishing the damn thing!

It was like giving birth. (From a male graduate!)

## Dissertation journeys

I suspect that for most of us, setting out to do a dissertation is like taking a trip into foreign territory. You've been on journeys before (all that essay-writing experience), but will this one be different? Thinking about however many thousands of words you have to write, suggests that this is likely to be a long trip.

Reading through the book you will find some unique TRAVELLERS' TIPS. These were the result of my request for 'recipes for success', Several students pointed out that there was no such thing but they all shared lots of helpful hints anyway. Their suggestions may help you through your dissertation, saving you time and energy, but as this person points out:

It's difficult to give a one, two, three approach to success. Each student is very much an individual.

Another used a 'journey metaphor' to describe her experience.

For me, the result is not as important as the process. It is the same thing as saying that in a journey the important thing is not the destination but the trip itself.

Whilst working on my dissertations I came across this poem, ITHAKA, written by the contemporary Greek poet, Cavafy. Perhaps you'll find some inspiration from it but in any case, I wish you 'bon voyage' on your unique dissertation journey.

As you set out for Ithaka
hope your road is a long one,
full of adventure, full of discovery.
...don't be afraid
...keep your thoughts raised high.

Hope your road is a long one.
May there be many summer mornings when,
with what pleasure, what joy,
you enter harbours you're seeing for the first time.

...so you're old by the time you reach the island,
wealthy with all you've gained along the way,
not expecting Ithaka to make you rich.

Ithaka gave you the marvellous journey.
Without her you wouldn't have set out.
She has nothing left to give you now.

And if you find her poor, Ithaka won't have fooled you.
Wise as you have become, so full of experience,
you'll have understood by then
what these Ithakas mean.[1]

# 1    What is a dissertation anyway?

**One student I met said 'nobody's told me what a dissertation is, so I don't know where to start.' Another got half-way through completing her questionnaire (and her dissertation) and found herself asking the question, 'What is a dissertation anyway?'**

One way to answer this question is to ask others who have written one as they have recently experienced the 'living meaning' behind these academic texts.

These responses, from 'novice' undergraduates who were about to start their work, show that many of us use the familiar to describe the unfamiliar.

It is a kind of long essay, four times as long as usual ones, but more formal.

A long essay looking at an issue from every angle you can think of and writing down your impressions, justifying them or criticising them from literature on, or other people's experiences of, the subject.

It's a long drawn out essay, usually with a conclusion at the end, but it is also a labour of love, doing research into something you are interested in.

It is not just a long essay. It takes many weeks or months of work, both researching and writing. It includes areas not in essays such as literature reviews. When complete it looks much like, in structure and style, a book.

Some students emphasise the research component of the task whilst others give a realistic appraisal of the time and effort involved.

> Although most people consider my unit to be a dissertation option, I think of it as a piece of empirical research with the added extra of writing a dissertation on top.

> To me a dissertation is lots of hard work. I'd say it's about choosing a topic you're interested in, doing lots of reading and in my case also empirical work, and then doing lots of writing in a very complicated academic style.

> It's very time-consuming, varied work which massively encroaches on other current studies and holiday periods!

These postgraduates, in defining 'the product' and 'the process', show diversity of opinion in their 'with hindsight' views.

> It is a book you write yourself.

> It's like your own baby.

> It is a summary of your abilities as an academic.

> It's a piece of work to be kept in perspective - an achievement whatever the mark - concrete evidence - indescribable!

> I don't see it as a 'finished product'....it is a piece of 'ourselves', creative, work of our hands and minds.

It has been stimulating and satisfying, although always hard work and often frustrating. You emerge from it like a 'phoenix rising from the flames'.

It has been a process of self-discovery as well as a discovery of other things, people, ideas. It is a learning process which although painful at some stages, it 'pays off in the end'.

It's not just academic learning and knowledge - it's everything! It's not only what you learn from the academic point of view. It's also about using computers, not being isolated, learning to work with other people - it's everything together.

It's been frustrating, messy, like stepping into the unknown, a test of skills and confidence; positive, sometimes excruciating, other times amazing - like nothing else!

It may be helpful (and revealing) to ask your tutor or supervisor for their version of 'What is a dissertation anyway?', particularly as there may be marked differences between disciplines. Or you can find your own answer - by doing one yourself - perhaps the best way of all.

## 2    Why choose to do a dissertation?

This chapter is based on responses to the question, 'Why did you choose to do a dissertation?' If dissertations may take many weeks or months of hard work, why do so many undergraduates undertake this academic task?

Although you may make a conscious decision to opt for this form of assessment, you are just as likely to find it is a compulsory requirement of your degree scheme - as was the case for **two-thirds** of the contributors to this book. You may feel that you are pushed into this situation, particularly if you are more at ease with exams, or you may welcome the chance to investigate a topic in depth. The responses of those who were able to choose are categorised as follows:

### Strategic approaches
- Aversion to/avoidance of exams
- Realisation of one's strengths
- Realistic consideration of workload

### Practical, personal, real-world concerns
- Access to data and resources
- Opportunity to travel
- Making use of personal experience
- Developing interest from coursework
- Chance to integrate 'real-world' concerns into study

### Freedom in learning
- Freedom to 'do your own thing'
- Being in control
- Test out suitability for postgraduate study
- Personal learning and creativity

## Strategic approaches

Aversion to exams can vary from mild dislike to abhorrence as these two responses show.

> Didn't fancy doing the exam.

> Spending three hours in an examination hall is the most illogical way of asking an individual to demonstrate his/her knowledge and understanding of a given topic.

Others suggest that a realistic awareness of their strengths and weaknesses was a contributing factor.

> I always did better in coursework than in exams so I thought a dissertation would improve my degree grade.

> I didn't feel confident that I would succeed in an exam on the subject - it was too wide and 'up in the air'. It seemed a good alternative to two essays and an exam.

Weighing up how best to manage their workload as a whole was an important factor for some students.

> Less pressure during finals.

> Mostly to avoid log jam of exams.

## Practical, personal, real-world concerns

Amongst the practical considerations, which some students identified as influential in their decision to undertake a dissertation, was the ready availability of data.

> I was teaching anyway and thus had data for a study.

> I had the personal diaries of my great, great, grandfather...a superb piece of primary history to use.

The opportunity to travel, or the possibility of making use of experience gained abroad, motivated others.

> I loved the idea of doing my own fieldwork observation and was desperately keen to go back to Brazil to do something.

> I wanted to travel to India and this was a good excuse!

> Doing a dissertation was a compromise really as I had hoped that going (abroad) would count as an 'enterprise unit'. Since it didn't, writing up my experiences was suggested as a way of academically validating them.

The notion of making use of personal interests and previous experience is a theme which recurs in several accounts.

> I chose to integrate personal experience with academic knowledge.

> I had a particular interest in the subject and felt it was important to research and analyse the area in some

depth, rather than fleetingly examining the issues in a shorter essay format.

The opportunity to develop academic interest arising from previous courses was a motivating factor for some people.

I chose to do this because I'd found the first year course interesting.

I was interested in pursuing the topic further, following up from a half-unit.

For others, the opportunity to integrate 'real-world' concerns provided a strong motive.

I wanted to bring 'outside of academic' interests into the content of my degree.

I was intrigued by the idea of producing something the museum might publish.

## Freedom in learning

Some said that they wanted to use the opportunity to develop additional dimensions to their degree, giving them freedom, control and self-direction.

The subject was not covered in any other courses in the department and I wanted to study it.

It was the opportunity to have more control over the result than if I'd taken an exam.

Possibly to do my own thing...not spoon-fed education.

I wanted a project with more freedom to explore my own interests.

Others wanted to use a dissertation as a testing ground for their suitability for postgraduate study in the future.

It is a way of finding out whether I can work all by myself.

It was useful in that it allowed me to do something which I was thinking about for a postgraduate course.

Issues of personal learning and creativity are echoed here.

It allows for individualism of expression and allowed me to combine creative writing and formal academic presentation.

Hopefully it will allow me to unlock some potential which the taught courses don't seem to touch.

## TRAVELLERS' TIPS on motivation

Study what interests you - enthusiasm is a great motivator and source of inspiration.

Doing a dissertation can be satisfying and fun. If I'd known how much I'd enjoy it, I would have done at least two others.

If in doubt, go for it - be extreme - don't hold back. It's your best chance to get your voice heard.

Believe in yourself and go for it!

Definitely do a dissertation if you get the chance - it's great to show to a potential employer as evidence of your individual skills and abilities.

Take a chance and do it
But.....don't do it if you're trying to give up smoking.

The basic fact that it's worth doing a dissertation. It shows you're capable of research and have good writing skills (and it looks good on your CV).

You should be convinced that you're doing something worthwhile, regardless of whether others approve, like or appreciate it. This is only possible if the 'you' in you is involved in the work.

# 3    Is it a good way of being assessed?

**This question was put to students who had finished their dissertation: 'Do you feel that doing a dissertation was a good way of assessing your abilities?'**

You might like to consider these responses at the outset of your work. Although some students had not yet been awarded a grade for their dissertation and the majority had undertaken the task as a compulsory requirement of their degree, their responses were overwhelmingly positive.

The only two negative answers were:

> Not really - I prefer exams because I find them less stressful.

> No, because the actual marking of a dissertation reflects the subjective opinion of the marker(s) anyway.

Many of those who did feel it was a good form of assessment, drew on their familiarity with exams or essays to make a comparison.

> It's better than short essays; much better than exams.

> Yes - it assessed your ability to work hard and not to remember facts as with exams.

Some indicated why they felt it was a good method of assessment.

Definitely much better than set pieces of coursework that have been answered over a thousand times before.

The dissertation process is a relatively slow and ongoing one, unlike exams which seem to entail how much you can remember and re-tell in three hours! Dissertations force you to try to make sense of the project and the process.

I had become tired with essays. Ideas can be developed more fully and creatively in dissertations.

Unlike an exam it tested more than memory. It assesses your understanding of topics.

It allowed me to acquire/maintain/enhance a very wide range of skills, eg. original research, library skills, essay-writing, critical reading and so on, which cannot be employed/tested in say, an exam. So I was assessed over a broad field rather than just three hours of thinking on your feet in exam situation.

Others felt that doing a dissertation provided an opportunity to realise their capabilities and to show these to an examiner.

It was my highest mark in my degree. It gave me the opportunity to show myself and the department what I am capable of.

For some, there was a more personal element of self-evaluation involved. They refer to personally significant learning as opposed to merely satisfying external requirements.

I feel much more sure of what I learned from it and that I will be assessed on that, rather than the 'chance' situation in exams.

It's possible to spot specific areas of learning and expertise one didn't have before.

It allowed a 'personality' to come through the work.

Definitely. The whole thing is yours, start to finish - I feel it indicates competence.

Two students seem to suggest that despite a natural inclination towards examinations (and the pressures involved) they had found they could adapt their way of working to dissertation-writing.

I can only work under pressure and so leaving the dissertation to the last minute certainly provided the pressure I needed!

Yes although my essays were never exceptional (my exams are better), I found dissertation writing was inspiring and worthwhile.

And finally, this response reminds us that doing a dissertation can also be regarded as an examination.

It's a major piece of work which requires all-round abilities. However, it is like doing a 100% exam really because you do put all your eggs in one basket - I only hope my supervisor was steering me in the right direction.

# TRAVELLERS' TIPS on assessment

Find out as much as you can about marking criteria.

Make sure you fully understand your marker's expectations.

On a practical level, don't read too much - you can't be examined on something that's still in your head.

Plan according to what your supervisor likes, at least to a certain extent (mine likes photographs!)

If the final mark is very important to you, then it might be very stressful. I don't really care about my mark now because I feel I did a good piece of work and I learned a lot, which is far more important.

Aim to hand it in and let go!

# 4    Selecting a topic

**Responses to the question, 'What motivated your choice of topic?' tend to overlap to some extent with those relating to an earlier question about general motivation. This suggests that the decision-making processes involved in choosing a topic tend to be quite complex.**

It may be that you have a topic in mind, and then you decide to do a dissertation (or, you discover that it is a compulsory requirement). Or, you may decide that you want to do a dissertation and only then do you think about possible topics. Or, you may find the topic evolves as a gradual coming together of several inter-related factors.

Nearly all of the contributors to this book were able to choose their own topic, though a few had to select from a topic list supplied by their department. Their wide-ranging responses reflect the great diversity that we now find amongst the student population. This range of backgrounds and abilities is acknowledged by those providing education at degree level.

> Students are no longer either privileged vessels to be filled full of knowledge, nor are they (for the most part) 'novitiates' of an 'academic priesthood'. They enter higher education with their own requirements, expectations and aspirations.[2]

A dissertation may be one of the few opportunities within a degree scheme for you to develop your own academic, vocational or personal interests. They may derive from prior experience or current concerns, they may relate to longer-term career plans, or they may be part of an ongoing commitment as a 'lifelong' learner.

According to this academic author, a dissertation 'can either be a rite de passage into the targeted discourse community or an exit qualification that enables the holder to leave the university world and enter another one'.[3]

Perhaps, like the majority of undergraduates, you intend to leave university after graduation to begin or resume a career. As a consequence, you may look for ways to integrate academic interests with issues of concern in the world 'outside' university. You may want to develop a range of skills and in-depth knowledge of a topic with which to impress a potential employer. Alternatively, and especially if you are intending to continue with postgraduate study, you may regard your dissertation journey as something more formal.

One postgraduate contributor summarised how he came to choose a topic for his MA dissertation.

> The dissertation was a compromise between who I was in the past, who I might become in the future, and where I was doing well in the present.

I have borrowed his themes of 'past', 'present', and 'future' to categorise others' responses. Whilst reading how they came to select their topic, you may find yourself asking, 'How might this dissertation serve my own needs and requirements?'

**The past**
- personal or professional experience
- prior interest in the topic
- extension of previous academic work

**The present**
- relevance to 'real-world' concerns
- interest encouraged by tutor/staff
- integration with other studies
- challenge, conviction and passion

**The future**
- career prospects
- personal growth
- opportunity for innovative research

## The Past

Many contributors were keen to draw on their personal or professional experience.

> I have worked for many years with individuals who have learning difficulties.

> I had lived and worked in a Jamaican school.

> I had experience of two approaches to faith during my time abroad and was interested in the role of the Christian faith as both spiritually and politically liberating.

For several others, doing a dissertation was an opportunity to develop their prior interest in a topic.

The topic had interested me for some time. I felt this gave me the opportunity to look at it more closely.

My topic is related to issues which are personally important to me.

Not surprisingly perhaps, some envisaged their dissertation as an extension of previous academic work.

Previous interest was stimulated by doing an essay on the subject in the second year.

I had done an assignment in a similar vein and wanted to expand on it.

It is based on my experiences during a previous piece of research which was submitted as a 'mini-project'.

## The Present

Many students indicated that their main priority in selecting a topic was that it should have some relevance to 'real world' concerns.

A desire to do something 'useful' however remote.

My concerns are prisoners for whom the ultimate punishment is to remove their means of communication.

Concern amongst local people at home and an interest in links between Public Health and the environment.

Personal interest in issues about HIV and AIDS, and a desire to extend my existing practical experience.

I am interested in conservation and the environment, particularly man's effect on woodland.

Tutors often encouraged their students to develop an interest in a particular area.

I was impressed with a lecturer's use of computers in the department and felt he might have a 'suitable project' - he did - and I'm trying to do it!

My topic developed from a point that one of the lecturers mentioned as an aside in a lecture.

I was encouraged to do this by staff in the department who sent me on a conference.

The possibility of integrating the dissertation topic with their other studies influenced some contributors.

This work complemented another dissertation I was doing on a related topic.

The particular Combined Major I'm doing leaves you in something of a void. I was eager to work in the 'middle ground'.

Challenge, conviction and passion aroused these people.

It was the determination to attempt a First Class pass.

Disagreement with previous work on the topic.

Faith in Christ and standing up for what is right.

I am passionately interested in the courses on which we place students and whether we put them on the right course.

## The Future

Career prospects were an important priority for some students.

I have an interest in speech therapy as a career.

This topic will hopefully enhance my job prospects for either the public or private sector.

Whereas, this undergraduate's motivation was linked to personal growth.

Hopefully I will learn more about myself as a person.

And lastly, others recognised the opportunity to be innovative.

I find these two topics interesting and this combination has never been researched before.

This particular topic was an unusual one with little research already done on it and therefore it appealed.

# TRAVELLERS' TIPS on choosing a topic

Be really interested in your chosen topic - your interest fires the enthusiasm you need to complete the work.

Enjoy the chance to involve yourself in a topic that inspires you - it's very important.

If possible, complement pieces of work so you're not involved in too many/diverse subject areas.

Pick a topic that won't bore you after six months!

On an idealistic level I would say try to enjoy your work by making it yours.

Find something that will still interest you as much at the end as the beginning - even the best ideas wear thin in February!

Choose a topic that you really like and so in the process of learning, you enjoy the whole thing. What you learn in the end is the real secret.

# 5    Feeling apprehensive?

**This chapter provides a realistic overview of how it really feels to face a new, and often daunting, task. It covers issues that conventional study skills books tend to gloss over and if you find that you identify with others' doubts and uncertainties, I guess it means you're fully human.**

As the range and sheer quantity of apprehensions presented here might discourage the faint-hearted from ever getting started on a dissertation, I'll begin with some words of reassurance. Most contributors mentioned three or four apprehensions but nobody experienced the whole lot! Neither did any of these factors prevent these students from getting on with their dissertations - and successfully completing them.

When I first read through these responses, I felt relieved that the things which had worried me were either very similar to others' concerns, or were not half as bad (like reading about the undergraduate who worried about sending out 2,500 questionnaires - my 59 seemed manageable after that!). I hope these accounts, which may at first sight seem overwhelming, will actually have a positive and reassuring effect on you too.

Although about half of the contributors to this study said that they were given clear guidelines, everyone, without exception, gave very full responses to a subsequent question about their apprehensions. One postgraduate's comment seems to characterise how most people were feeling.

> We were given some guidelines but I still felt insecure about many things.

This raises the question of whether departmental guidelines are of real value to students? Perhaps much depends on what information is given and whether it is so prescriptive as to inhibit creativity. Although I believe we have a right, as with any other academic task, to be given explicit criteria and clear information about departmental requirements, such guidelines are unlikely to provide a panacea to cover all eventualities. Perhaps they tend to act as a kind of 'comfort blanket'?

Apprehensions about the task tend to fall under four broad headings:

## Personal
- General fears
- Self-doubt

## Expectations
- What is expected?
- Assessment requirements

## Time Management

## Task-related factors
- Data collection and analysis
- Size/content
- Reviewing literature
- Structure/format/style

## Personal factors

These apprehensions reveal the underlying fears disclosed by many of the people I spoke to.

I had a general fear about doing something I had never done before.

As far as I know, no-one else had ever written about this before. I kept worrying my whole idea was crazy.

I'm frightened to death of making a mess of it.

Self-doubt was a very common factor.

I'm worried about being academic.

Will I be able to produce a dissertation that is of some relevance ie. not just a load of information that leads to no real conclusion?

Dissertations I had looked at seemed like books - this petrified me!

## Expectations

These responses reflect much of the underlying anxiety experienced by many contributors.

I wasn't too sure what the department was expecting from me, especially to what degree depth and detail were required.

I knew what I wanted to do and say, so I put my dissertation together by myself, but I still felt uncertain as to what would be expected.

A lack of explicit criteria concerned several others.

> The course was very open-ended and there were no particular criteria set about presentation, content, even methodology which made it more difficult.

> Although the department produces a leaflet on guidelines for essay-writing, there is apparently no such information for dissertations - not even to say how long they should be. Consequently most information was picked up from other students.

> I was given no information about presentation, only that it should have a title and a course number.

This postgraduate spoke at length about his concerns.

> I sense that there are some very basic things that don't get imparted. I feel this is part of the business of 'jumping through hoops'. There is a gap between tutors and students and part of that gap has to do with freedom. Tutors want to leave you responsible for deciding what the framework and format of your dissertation is. Nevertheless, in the end, I feel there are fairly clear criteria about what is acceptable and maybe guidelines could have been more specific.

A great many people voiced their uncertainty about the standards that would be required, as well as expressing their ignorance of marking criteria.

> Are tutors expecting a 'higher' standard than from essays?

I knew nothing about marking criteria, only that it would be marked by the external examiner.

Will topic choice somehow determine my grade?

I realise that not all dissertations are the same but I needed some sort of starting point....I know the department doesn't like to be prescriptive but it needs to be when it comes to evaluation.

I still don't understand the marking criteria (but that goes for essays and exams as well!)

Each supervisor/course tutor seemed to have slightly different marking criteria.

When considering how their dissertation might be marked, a few people drew attention to a potential conflict between the product and the process.

Is it the 'taking part' or the result that is most important, or a combination of both?

I suspect that a dissertation is evaluated mainly on the basis of the product, the finished form, and not on what has gone into it.

## Time Management

Nearly all contributors mentioned worries about time management in their responses.

I started and completed my dissertation in about four weeks (I always work cramming-style) but my nervousness and uncertainty put me off getting on with the task.

I'm worried about the pressure of essays, presentations and exams, as well as balancing family responsibilities.

I was really worried that I would not be able to cope with the dissertation and with coursework and would have to scrap it and do the exam.

My apprehensions are that I will not finish it in time or that because I have to do it in my final year (whilst I have a lot of other academic commitments) it will not be as good as I had otherwise hoped.

Would I have the self-discipline to manage my time sensibly? (in the event I didn't).

## Task-related factors

Many anxieties about research methods and the handling of data surfaced in these accounts. General doubts were expressed about how to carry out the research.

Whether to go completely quantitative or to include qualitative research?

The hypothesis - how do I develop one?

I wasn't sure whether the methods I had used were ethnographical or case study etc. Terminology was a bit confusing.

My supervisor pointed me in the direction of all sorts of empirical studies but I couldn't really identify with these as they were mainly large scale studies. I felt I was just not equipped because the course had not been designed sufficiently for me to have developed those research skills by that stage.

Others feared that problems might arise out of their data collection methods.

My original apprehension was how to go about starting to do my own interviews.

I am apprehensive about going out into the 'field' collecting data. I'm not sure how accurate it should be.

I was slightly worried that I'd been over-ambitious in sending out 2,500 questionnaires but I was assured (rightly) by my supervisor and other members of staff that this would not present a problem.

And finally, there were apprehensions about data analysis.

At the moment I have a great deal of tedious analysis to plough through - and in some ways I feel I am not sure what I am looking for.

I was apprehensive that I had too much data - I didn't know whether to analyse it all superficially or to select some and analyse it in depth.

The sheer size of the task and the length of the dissertation was a daunting prospect for some people.

I thought I would never complete what I perceived to be an enormous task.

I'd never attempted length above 2,500 before.

For others, it was the scope that was daunting - they worried about how to focus their topic.

How am I going to decide on one aspect of the topic to concentrate on? And how to condense my information and get rid of irrelevant information.

Bringing my ideas across (saying important things; leaving out unimportant stuff).

General fears about the content of the dissertation occupied the thoughts of many contributors.

I was a little uncertain about the content of my dissertation and wasn't sure what I was going to do until I actually started working on it.

At first I was concerned I would not have enough information and at the end I worried I had too much!

I feel that the content was part of the process ie. the subject area shifted, to a degree, as I became more involved....I needed the freedom and flexibility to become fully involved with the subject matter.

How to incorporate their reading was a worry for others.

I'm already half-way through my project but I have not yet done any specific reading.

How much background reading is required? (I've done quite a lot, but how much should be put back into the dissertation?)

My supervisor suggested that I should 'look for something' on a topic and I said yes, but then thought, yes but where? how? - in the library? I felt awkward about this because maybe I was supposed to know.

The literature review provoked specific worries.

The part which scared me the most was the literature review - I wasn't quite sure what was required.

Everybody was talking about it - it's easy, it's difficult - so I thought they must know what it is, but I wasn't exactly sure. So I deduced more or less... but nobody gave us a definition and when I came here to do a Masters I had never come across this term.

Several contributors voiced their uncertainties about how to structure their dissertation.

I am unclear as to the difference between an extended essay and a dissertation.

Structure was the most daunting - when dealing with a wide subject everything ties in to everything else and making it 'linear' seemed daunting.

I was very apprehensive about the format - I wanted some sort of skeleton plan of the sections a dissertation should contain.

Some were advised to look at past dissertations to help them learn how to structure a dissertation. Others missed this opportunity.

If you look at past dissertations you can begin to see what they all have in common. Others' outstanding dissertations can provide inspiration. They all share focus and coherence - they share a sense that all the parts are working towards a particular end.

We were constantly told to look at old dissertations - I didn't find this helpful. I looked at many, maybe good, maybe bad - no way to tell. I think it would have been helpful if three or four good dissertations were selected to represent different ways of doing dissertations.

Past dissertations - I didn't think of doing this until late on - my supervisor assumed (wrongly) that I knew about conventions and structure but I didn't.

Undergraduate dissertations are not readily available in the department and there are no copies in the library either.

A few people mentioned apprehensions about the style of writing that would be required.

I was always worried about conventions because it is easy to become 'carried away' in a big project - if you make it look too much like you're 'enjoying yourself', style becomes journalistic and popular and too informal. This had happened to me before with essays so the danger seemed even greater with a dissertation.

I was unsure whether essay-style writing was adequate for a dissertation - was it academic enough?

I am uncertain of what style to use in writing - detached, narrative, descriptive, involved?

This postgraduate was concerned about writing in her second language.

Writing in English, from the language and the cultural point of view, was problematic - because when I use my own language I write in a different way, such as very long paragraphs. Also I had to change certain terminology because the connotations of the terms were very different to those associated with the words in British culture.

And one last apprehension of a practical kind.

Finding someone to type it for me might be a problem!

# TRAVELLERS' TIPS on managing time

Do bits over the year and enjoy it. If you do, I feel it shows through your work.

Make your own schedule and stick to it.

Review progress regularly.

Set aside three to six weeks to get it out of the way.

If you can, start your dissertation over the summer vacation so that when you get back in October you have a foundation to work on.

Divide the dissertation into manageable parts, as finishing one part motivates you onto the next.

Aim to finish at least two weeks before deadline. Last minute rushes seem to cost my friends a lot of marks.

Be careful of burnout.

Don't leave everything to the last minute, especially if you need the university's computer system - it has a habit of crashing at the worst possible moments.

Set yourself goals ie write intro by Friday.

Don't panic! It'll all come together in the end.

# 6    How do you choose a supervisor?

**In this chapter students reveal how they went about choosing someone to supervise their work as well as sharing some of their experiences of this one-to-one relationship.**

My own interest to discover what thoughts occupy others when faced with the prospect of working with a supervisor was initially inspired by a tutor's advice to a group of undergraduates; he considered that the **only** important consideration was to **choose an expert** in the area of your topic. When asked whether it was necessary to 'get on' with that person the tutor seemed unable to grasp the rationale behind the question. Some of us seemed to feel intuitively that interpersonal skills might be more crucial in a supervisory relationship than in lectures and seminars.

Not all the contributors to this book were able to choose their supervisor. Of the 63% who had been able to make a free choice, those who had completed their dissertation were given a checklist and asked to indicate those factors which had been most influential in their decision. The following emerged as the highest ranked factors:

|  | **Student response** |
|---|---|
| **Genuine shared interest** (in topic) | 84 % |
| **Academic expertise** (specific to topic) | 68 % |
| **Enthusiasm** | 64 % |
| Past experience of good working relationship | 60 % |
| Empathy | 48 % |
| Shared socio-political views | 44 % |
| Inter-personal/communication skills | 40 % |

Several students mentioned the advantages of having various types of contact with their supervisor.

> I think it is crucial to have had contact with a supervisor before starting a dissertation ie. discussion of other assignments, collaboration in seminars and probably some contact socially.

> I feel it is important to be able to meet your supervisor, not just with polished work, but also with ideas, requests for advice and friendly chats.

Other significant factors were also mentioned.

> I was impressed by her ability to criticise without offending ie. to encourage rather than put down - ie. confidence-building.

> She was honest and supportive but offered challenge and was open to students exploring boundaries (personal and academic) within their work.

> He shares my belief that creativity, originality and deep thinking are more important than regurgitating other people's opinions.

Those who had completed their dissertation (and survived the experience of supervision) were asked if, with hindsight, their criteria had changed in any way. Most indicated that the same would still apply but they tended to re-emphasise the importance of shared interest and enthusiasm.

No change as such, but confirmation that a shared interest is a major advantage even if you are coming from a different perspective/angle than the supervisor.

Enthusiasm and a genuine interest are vital if you are to enjoy researching and writing your dissertation and also if you are to feel confident about expressing your opinion.

One postgraduate thought that the interest should be in the student rather than in the chosen topic.

Supervisors need to have a genuine interest in their students.

For another, personality was an over-riding factor.

Personality is crucial - far more than expertise in the topic area.

Others identified a combination of expertise in the topic together with personal characteristics.

Clarity, empathy, interest in research topic and knowledge in your topic area.

I had the supervisor who was an expert on my topic and furthermore (luckily enough) she was extremely supportive, patient and understanding.

For these contributors, the ability to direct, without being over-directive, was a desirable quality in a supervisor.

> I liked the fact that he did not try to structure it for me
> - I was given a lot of freedom - suggestions were only
> given when asked.

> I worked alone because I had no option but am now
> glad I did. Friends doing supervised dissertations had
> lecturers practically telling them the directions in
> which they must go. I think it is crucial that you
> choose a supervisor who will allow you to explore
> your topic in your way.

However, one person would have preferred rather more, not
less, direction.

> Supervisor was not very helpful - I went full of ideas,
> hoping he would help me pick the best, most
> manageable, ones and he didn't.

## Postgraduates' experiences

The following selection of more in-depth comments are drawn
from conversations with postgraduates engaged in writing MA
dissertations. I suspect that undergraduates may also identify
with some of their experiences.

> I don't really know if I chose my supervisor or not. It
> came about through general discussion of the topic
> area with a lecturer. I drafted a proposal which she
> approved and I then assumed she was going to be my
> supervisor. I suppose I chose her, but it was an
> assumption rather than a clearly negotiated
> arrangement over which I had some control. It just
> kind of happened.

In the beginning I had some doubts and needed advice but as time went on I realised I could find the answers myself as I felt more independent.

I don't want to convey the impression that I needed to be guided by my supervisor throughout. In fact, it was just the opposite. It was more that I needed to talk to other people and to listen. It was not that I needed a supervisor telling me what to do, because if they had done that it would have had the opposite effect.

I realise that my first consideration was to look at my supervisor as a person, and then to ask myself whether he would really be able to help or not. Besides being top-notch in one's area, a supervisor is equally important, if not more so, as a person. I think this human aspect is crucial.

## 'Novices' - in anticipation of supervision

Those students who were just embarking on their dissertation journey were asked whether they had chosen a supervisor, and, if so, how they had made that choice. Some who had received the questionnaire during the summer vacation were still rather confused.

I'm not sure if I shall be allocated a supervisor or whether I get to choose one myself.

I don't know yet, but I do think that the supervisors should have been appointed before the vacation.

Novices tended to highlight similar issues to those raised by recent graduates and MA students. For some, the research topic itself was the deciding factor.

> He was the only one in the department whose specialised subjects are anything near what I wanted to study.

> Your topic area 'selects' your tutor. Therefore if your preferred area is popular, that supervisor may have a limited capacity re. number of students taken. I had to adapt my project in order to suit another supervisor whose interests were in a different direction.

For a few others, more personal characteristics were emphasised.

> I've chosen someone who I respect and who is on the same wavelength as me.

> Obviously I would like a supervisor whom I got on well with and felt able to discuss problems with and especially one that was on campus most of the time.

The majority of contributors mentioned their supervisor's academic expertise in the topic area together with some other factor. Many included the notion of being able to 'get on' with the person.

> Someone who is easy to talk to and who is prepared to give time for discussion at the various stages. (I wanted to avoid a supervisor I had for a previous project as I found him difficult to talk to though he is an excellent lecturer).

Knowledge about the area, generally helpful, interested in what I was doing anyway, and I get on well with him.

He has worked on similar topics before. Also we get along well - he lets me use my own ideas.

The same undergraduates were also invited to share how they thought their supervisor might be able to help them as their work progressed.

I hope she will provide me with some pointers for reading.

Guidance over the best ways of going about things - reading, carrying out fieldwork - and to give support.

To give constructive criticism. To advise on research techniques and to actually read drafts.

Help on what should go in, what not; hopefully some help on how to set it out.

Encouragement to look at aspects/areas that I have failed to consider. Most of all an honest opinion.

To give me hints on how to proceed if I get stuck.

Telling me I can do it when I feel swamped!

You may remember that at the start of this chapter I suggested that 'getting on' with the person might be an important pre-requisite in a supervisory relationship and this does seem to be supported by the responses of many contributors. However doing a supervised dissertation seems to involve learning to discuss and develop one's own ideas, and to accept constructive criticism and this may only be achieved through effective communication by both parties. In other words, the 'getting on with a supervisor' may be an integral part of the learning process rather than a pre-requisite.

A working party of the Society for Research into Higher Education, which was set up twenty years ago to investigate project methods, gave the following advice to tutors supervising undergraduates:

> It is important to be aware of the student's relative maturity and ability and be ready to respond with enthusiasm, challenge, critical discussion and most of all, encouragement.[4]

But they also gave this warning:

> The lecturer may be shy, absorbed in his own research, impatient of student demands, a habitual dampener of enthusiasm, or just plain lazy.....it may be good for the students to realise that lecturers are only human.[5]

This recent graduate's comment may alert you to heed your own instincts if you are aware of a potentially problematic relationship, and, if necessary, to consider some alternative.

> One of my supervisors was a pain. I knew he was a pain in the beginning but I did not think it would matter - it did. I found myself being totally confused by what he wanted...in the end I produced something

that was schizophrenic and paid the price in the final marks.

## Friends and allies?

Fortunately, moves to improve the effectiveness of learning and teaching in higher education include a recent report which promotes the idea of students and supervisors as 'friends and allies', as described in this quote:

> There are significant rewards for making the supervisor-student relationship as much as possible into an affair of peers. This permits the creation of a 'we' culture, involved in a shared enterprise. This in turn gives moral support to the student, and sometimes a reciprocal stimulation of ideas. A 'we' culture can be achieved to a surprising degree, even though the student will be aware that they have a formal examination to pass and you as supervisor do not. It is a matter of creating equality in the way of personal respect whilst accepting a difference of role.[6]

Whether you are supervised by an academic with forward-looking ideas, or one who takes a more traditional approach, it seems that your decision is likely to be based, to some extent, on individualistic, and therefore somewhat unpredictable, factors. You may be fortunate to regard your supervisor as someone who becomes a 'friend and ally', or to feel that you have been apprenticed to a master of his/her craft, but such an inspirational relationship may be an added bonus rather than a foregone conclusion.

You may well ask, 'But what if I'm doing a compulsory dissertation and have no choice about who will supervise my work?'. This may present more of a challenge but it is likely that your supervisor will have a genuine interest and/or expertise in the research topic, and will have been appointed on that basis; most students have highlighted these as important ingredients. Perhaps reading through others' insights may give you ideas as to how to work from this foundation to create a collaborative culture, if that is what you feel will help.

You could always recommend this book to your supervisor as a way of helping him or her to think about supervision from the learner's perspective - it could provide the stimulus for an interesting discussion.

In closing this chapter, I feel it is important to mention that quite a few contributors seemed to have got on with their dissertation with little or no help from supervisors. Although some appeared to be showing their preference to work independently, others' reasons were not disclosed in this study.

# TRAVELLERS' TIPS on supervision

If you can, choose your supervisor with care.

Find a tutor you can work with and be open with.

Get a good supervisor and believe your dissertation will work.

Talk to your tutors. Remember they're on your side.

Have confidence in yourself - only allowing a supervisor to assist you and not lead. It's easy to be intimidated by their knowledge and expertise.

Don't choose one who's a 100% perfectionist!

In order for your supervisor to be able to help you, it is essential that you share what you've done, tried to do, or the point at which you're stuck.

Supervision depends not only on the supervisor but also on the student.

# 7    Who else might help?

**Having looked at some of the ways in which a supervisor may help you with your dissertation, I now review other sources of support and guidance which others have found helpful.**

Only a few undergraduates received any formal instruction through departmental seminar groups. However, some contributors who had participated in a 'Writing a Dissertation' course, run by Lancaster's Summer University, were enthusiastic in recommending this to others; their disappointment seemed to lie in the fact that their own departments and universities had failed to provide a preparatory course in term time.

It is noticeable, in the responses which follow, that no undergraduates mentioned any formal group support. This suggests that, in general, formalised 'network groups' or 'peer sets' are not a common provision for undergraduates. In contrast, most postgraduates said that participating in research groups had helped them through their dissertation work. It does seem that undergraduates are encouraged, or at least not actively discouraged, to take an isolated approach, whilst postgraduates are helped to work collaboratively.

Many students relied on informal support from their friends and peers, as well as help and guidance from staff other than their supervisor.

## Moral support
* other students
* friends and family
* support groups (postgraduates only)

## Academic guidance
- staff other than supervisor
- departmental seminars

## Moral support

These contributors appreciated help from their peers.

> So far the greatest help has been from fellow students who question, encourage and assist with statistics. This mutual support seems invaluable.

> Friends at university were invaluable in going over ideas and in directing me to articles they had seen which related to my topic.

Friends and family were a lifeline for others.

> Support from my partner when I needed it most - in times of despair.

> My friends supported me when I felt really low and persuaded me to seek appropriate advice when I had difficulties.

Postgraduates shared their experience of research groups.

> The research groups were useful as I could discuss a problem and ask what others thought. I found another person whose research was in the same field so we talked a lot with each other. I didn't feel isolated as it is a collaborative approach.

Seminars were helpful - because it was nice to know someone cared and it helped a lot to share problems. When I explained my work to other people it somehow clarified the ideas for me.

## Academic guidance

Some people discovered guidance and help from staff other than their supervisor.

A lecturer was very helpful in directing me to sources, though it was only by chance that I'd even got to talking about my dissertation. My dissertation tutor was not so helpful and I wished I'd known the other lecturer had an interest in the topic as I would have asked him to be my tutor.

A lecturer from another department was particularly helpful - he even lent me one of his own books.

Seeing a tutor who specialises in study skills allowed me to explore the connections between thinking, writing, speaking, ideas, analysing, critique etc. After seeing her I started to approach and write work in a different way - that is, from the middle of the muddle!

Just a few undergraduates mentioned departmental seminars which they had found useful.

We were put into dissertation tutorial groups - four students to a member of staff. The member of staff was not necessarily your supervisor - we were allocated the group alphabetically. I found the general advice about writing the dissertation was quite helpful.

We were given a series of lectures on embarking on a dissertation - the department went to great lengths to help prepare us for this and this help was invaluable.

The practicals and lectures in the second year were aimed at skills needed for dissertations.

One conclusion that may be drawn from these responses is that students appear to derive a lot of support and guidance from people who are not acting in a supervisory role. Mutual peer support seems to be of particular value which suggests that students may well be a valuable but under-utilised resource with regard to project and dissertation work. Perhaps the semi-formal research groups which seem to work well for postgraduates might be a collaborative method which could also be beneficial to you.

# TRAVELLERS' TIPS on getting help

Ask other students who have done a dissertation. The realities are often very different from the theories found in books.

Get together with others in whatever way suits you best.

Talk to as many people as possible who will listen. If necessary, become a bore.

Write to anybody, everybody - authors of books They can expand on what they say in a book and it can look impressive in your references (showing initiative).

Look around the whole university for tutors who may know something about your topic - there are often specialists in the most unpredictable places.

Find any postgrads who are undertaking work on a similar line - they may be willing to tell you all the problems at first hand and how to avoid them.

# 8    What are the pitfalls?

Earlier, in Chapter 5, apprehensions were shared - now for those problem areas which actually proved to be difficult during the process of doing a dissertation. All those who had completed their work were asked:

**What did you find most difficult about doing a dissertation? What caused you the most pain and anguish?**

Their experiences suggest these common pitfall areas.

## Getting started
- Time and motivation
- Self-doubt and lack of confidence

## Getting stuck
- Maintaining confidence or enthusiasm

## Writing
- Self discipline
- Focus, structure, argument
- Drafts, word processing
- Length
- Deadlines

## Disappointment
- Supervision
- Conflict of interests
- Limitations of research

## Getting started

> Starting it was a problem! It was resolved for me by leaving it so late that the pressure to complete it forced me into it in the end.

> Getting started was the hardest part - my tutor didn't seem to realise I was asking for help by taking pathetic chapter titles to her - I was really lost.

> Choosing the actual topic was difficult in the first place but once I got started it was fine.

Several students expressed self-doubts which prevented them from getting started.

> I found it difficult to have confidence in myself - fear of failure prevented me from getting on with it.

> I didn't really know how to practically organise my dissertation and not realising this, failed to get help early on which would have made the process easier.

> I felt utterly daunted by the scale of this work and have often doubted my own ability to dance words onto paper in an interesting and/or sensitive way.

> Fear of flunking the course paralysed me. I just had to write it and therefore tried to be positive and brave. Positive affirmations helped - and sheer bravado!

> I felt incompetent and unable to reach the standards of academic writing which would 'sound' professional, mature, relevant. It was a lack of self-confidence.

## Getting stuck

Although getting started was a problem for some, many others found it hard to keep going; maintaining confidence and enthusiasm were common problems.

I'm feeling very muddled - a feeling of not quite knowing if I'm doing it right.

I'm struggling to remember why I'm doing what I'm doing.

I'm feeling rather barren at the moment and have lost lots of enthusiasm. Trying to do it over the summer months was disastrous. Now I'm back at Uni I might be able to get it finished - if I'm disciplined enough.

I'm finding it difficult to envisage that this work will (hopefully) one day be an interesting piece of work.

I can't convince myself that what I'm doing is a credible piece of research.

I have at present come to a bit of a standstill. I'm starting to lose my enthusiasm for it all now and just want to get it out of the way as soon as possible. It's very difficult to keep the drive and eagerness when there are so many set-backs along the way.

## Writing

Actually starting to write was a major difficulty.

Just the usual problem of getting pen to paper!

I felt I needed to know where I was going (ie conclusion) before I began writing but couldn't know that until I began writing.

Writing it up - I didn't sleep much. To resolve the problem I allocated time and forced myself to do it - it got done!

Psychologically, 10,000 words seemed unachievable.

Writing the first draft was very stressful, converting vague ideas and rough notes into coherent text.

Undergraduates and postgraduates alike found difficulty in deciding on a focus for their work.

It was difficult keeping it under control. It was easy to digress and get diverted.

Having to home in on one topic was often very hard - hated the feeling I'd left so much interesting stuff out!

Focusing - you start with an idea, you read around the field and your idea soon grows into a 'monster' - the difficulty comes in cutting it down to size.

Structuring the dissertation was another common problem area.

I found it difficult to make it interesting and give it cohesiveness, rather than leaving it as a shapeless mass of information.

Difficulties in planning ie. what to include, in how much detail, under what heading/subheading.

Many people also found difficulties in structuring an argument.

In my department it must be demonstrated that the theoretical content is clearly understood, just referencing it is not enough. So, the project becomes more complicated than essays; especially in the 'tightening-up' stage of the argument structure.

Argument - the fears of it being non-academic and having no one specific argument. The lack of confidence wasn't resolved per se, but I did create an attitude of 'what's done is done' and hoped for the best!!

For me, argument was the most difficult - organising and arranging ideas teeming in my mind and trying to make them coherent and putting them on paper.

I had problems in structuring the argument and the piece of work. Although I can write sentences in a linear string, I find that instead of coming out as a coherent paragraph it comes out as a string of connections.

Submission of written drafts for feedback was helpful to some but disconcerting for others.

> I was a little shocked when my tutor told me to shorten the first draft - this meant I had to choose what to put in and what to leave out - even though I had already done a lot of work on it.

> As I wrote I found out what I wanted to say. It took a long time and a lot of revision - my supervisor helped by reading my drafts.

> Mainly I like to keep my supervisor at arms' distance from work in progress, but welcome and value her constructive criticisms as each section is written.

> I asked people with little background knowledge in the subject to read my draft and comment on its coherence.

Several mentioned practical difficulties with word processing their dissertation.

> The problem of a very practical sort - typing it up. For those who are typing-up themselves, it's worth remembering that the computer centre system often break down - so make back-up copies.

> Getting the dissertation printed caused the most anguish. To get it laser-printed without interruption, I used the computer lab at eight o' clock in the morning.

> Not having my own computer was a problem.

Once having started writing, some faced the difficulty of knowing when to stop.

> I thought I might get penalised for twice the amount of words.

> The dissertation had to be 12,500 words but I didn't get around to counting the words until five days before the dissertation was due. I found I had 25,000 words! It became a piece of unwriting - it was like gutting a fish or skinning a rabbit. It was like being in a lift on the 100th floor when the cable snaps, and watching the floors flick past, faster and faster. Every bit of extra writing and thought I'd put into it during the previous month just disappeared. I think this pitfall must have happened to someone else.

These contributors experienced difficulty towards the end.

> Endless checking and re-checking, ensuring references and bibliography are complete/accurate.

> I had a problem meeting the deadline! It became very rushed and I nearly gave up in the last week.

> Lack of time meant I spent many nights without sleep. I muddled through and friends helped me by chatting in my low moments.

## Disappointments

> The most difficult was having to express my, what I thought were original, ideas to a tutor who was less than positive because this approach did not comply

with his own methods of analysis. This negative feedback ruined my self-confidence. I resolved the problem...but by this point, I was so convinced I would receive a low mark anyway I just wanted to finish it.

In the dissertation where I found the supervisor problematic, I found myself being totally confused by what he wanted. I tried to resolve this by adapting my work to incorporate what he wanted but in the process my work lost some direction, and I paid the price in the final marks.

This undergraduate expressed her concern about a conflict between her own interests and those of her interviewees.

I think the people I interviewed expected me to 'fight their cause', when really I was trying to achieve a reasonable mark which would go towards my degree.

A postgraduate student reflected on her negative feelings after completing her work.

My supervisor kept reminding me that my research was meaningful but I felt frustrated that I had not found a way of communicating my findings to the community from which my data was drawn. I became quite pessimistic but perhaps others who are planning their research might be able to arrange feedback at the planning stage.

## TRAVELLERS' TIPS on pitfalls

Just get started without thinking too much about the task ahead. Do a bit at a time, chapter by chapter.

If I felt like cat-napping I did - often ideas came during those naps.

Write your ideas down, however small.

Don't let the blank page dictate a beginning, a middle and an end.

Think of the words in terms of 1,000 word blocks rather than as a panic-inducing 10,000 word whole.

It helped to ask myself 'What story am I telling?' 'Why?' and 'How did I get to it?'

Tell a story - crucial in keeping your mind on a central thread that will run through your work and make the final parts relevant to earlier parts.

Be flexible - modify plans and objectives if necessary.

Get a strong outline and stick to it.

Another student talked to me about reaching a moment when he took authorial control and started writing for himself. I found this inspiring.

I was told to divide mine into six areas and to write it like a book, with each section different, but clearly related to and expanding on previous sections.

Make the links and connections. Signpost where you're coming from and where you're going.

Writing up and presentation take far longer than the actual work so don't underestimate the time needed. I wrote mine in three weeks and then spent eight weeks typing it up.

Presentation (binding, printing, spelling) is really important. It biases the marker towards you from the start. It may seem trivial but it shows you've made the effort to impress.

# 9    Is it worth it in the end?

In this chapter, contributors share what they personally got out of doing a dissertation. All those who had completed their work were asked:

'What gave you the most pleasure and satisfaction in doing a dissertation?'

Their responses:

- Finishing / handing in the finished product
- Sense of achievement
- Confidence/ self-development
- Knowledge/ learning
- Originality
- Freedom
- Research experience
- Satisfaction through writing

You can sense the obvious relief and sense of pride that many felt on completing their work.

Finishing the damn thing!

Hell of a buzz when it's completed!

Seeing the final piece bound, with illustrations and front cover design. I didn't really want to part with it.

The department didn't insist that it was typed up, but it was worth having it typed because the presentation made such a difference.

Undoubtedly it was the final product, getting it bound; it looked so impressive, though it remains to be seen if the content matches the exterior gloss.

Actually producing the final bound thesis, with all my work presented to the best of my ability.

Watching it build up on disk on my computer and the final presentation - it's your own work - something individual to you.

However, for some there was more to it than just submitting a product for marking - the dissertation represented significant personal and/or academic achievement.

It was the feeling that I was doing a substantial piece of work that was all mine! Also giving it in - a big wad of laser-printed paper - very satisfying!

Carrying out original research, contact with local people, writing with a view to publication for the general public.

Feeling that I had completed a 'good' piece of work which was - to all intents and purposes - all my own, right from the original idea.

I felt very satisfied to have written what was effectively a short book. It was well worth doing.

Flicking through the final copy just prior to handing it in. Pure ego, I know, but it was a sense of achievement from setting out to create an academic work.

There was a great sense of satisfaction amongst those who felt that their work had been particularly worthwhile.

> It was an opportunity to validate lived, practical experience, rather than just regurgitating others' textbooks. While writing the dissertation some of the people have died, so that it now represents my loving and respectful acknowledgement of their lives.

> I felt I'd completed a substantial project and a worthwhile investigation of the relationship between a medical condition and industrial pollution.

> Knowing I was expressing concerns of people unable to do so themselves and finding something that other people seemed to find genuinely interesting and of some worth.

Others shared how their self-confidence had grown through doing their dissertation.

> I realised how much I was learning about myself, about others, about research and academic writing; I felt that I was developing - my thoughts, ideas and perceptions - they became more focused and mature through the writing and correcting process.

> The marks were more than I'd hoped for - this gave me a lovely boost of confidence.

> I gained confidence from being able to give some shape to my work - by structuring I felt a great sense of freedom and pride.

It has given me more understanding and insights into what my role should be when I go back to my professional work. It has given me clarity, direction and plans for the future.

The learning process was a specific point mentioned by several contributors. For some this was acquisition of new knowledge, whereas for others it was less tangible.

I enjoyed doing the bibliography and realising how much knowledge I had taken in.

It was the satisfaction of the learning and the hunger for more.

For me, it was the learning process - what I learned from it - but not just from the academic point of view - it was everything that I learned in the process.

Some commented on their satisfaction in creating an original piece of work.

Not writing stupid essays that thousands of others have written.

Creating something original that no one else had written about.

Others experienced a sense of liberation.

I enjoyed being controversial and 'way out' - the more 'open' style of a dissertation lets you do this.

The chance to work on your own ideas, with your own initiative, and show that you have good ideas, valid points and a systematic development of thought - very satisfying.

Having the opportunity to say what I wanted to say about a topic - not constrained by an essay title or bound by the confines of a course syllabus

Several admitted that their greatest pleasure had derived from the research process itself - either in collecting or analysing the data.

Being 'out there' - doing the interviews, meeting and talking to people.

Analysing data was like having something to play with.

Without question the data gave the most satisfaction. I spent a whole month on the analysis - it was really exciting - I could happily go back to the analysis even now!

Transcribing the tapes was very soothing.

Some seemed pleasantly surprised to find they actually enjoyed the writing (once they'd started!).

The writing-up process gave me confidence to embark on another dissertation.

Writing the final chapter and conclusions was satisfying; it was the time when I realised that I did actually have a coherent argument.

Once I was writing, immersing myself in a subject that really excited me was a pleasure.

The last few words I wrote felt amazing. I had achieved what I thought was impossible.

I hope you will draw inspiration from reading others' accounts of the pleasure that derived from their work - especially if you have read through the previous chapters in which they revealed so many apprehensions and difficulties - the muddle from which they wondered if they, and their dissertation, would ever escape. They have emerged, in the words of one contributor, 'like a phoenix rising from the flames.'

## 10    A personal summary

When I think back to my first attempts at dissertations (which is not very long ago), I realise that two major assumptions were made. Firstly, tutors seemed to assume that I knew what to do (which convinced me that I should know), and secondly, I made the assumption that everyone else knew what to do. Both these assumptions were false. I experienced the isolation of 'working in the dark' but, as this book now shows, my experience was not unique. Others have also experienced confusion and uncertainty.

Talking things through with others made my life easier, even though, as the contributors to this book have shown, doing a dissertation is a very individualistic enterprise. So much seems to depend on you as a person, your interests, your goals, your motivation and your learning strategies. Much may also depend on the subject area you are studying, your department and your examiners. The topic you choose, the way you go about researching and writing up your work, the kind of supervisory relationship that you want to create, how you organise yourself and your study - all these factors are incredibly variable.

There is no blueprint - no 'recipe for success'. What suits one student may be worthless advice for another. I am, however, convinced of the benefits of critical reflection, both on the views of the 'experts' and on the 'insider approach' of learners. And of course, of the need to communicate with each other.

Having said there is no blueprint, I'm now going to offer a personal 'checklist' of the tips which inspired me the most. Perhaps you will generate a list from your own experiences and those of friends?

- Doing a dissertation can be satisfying and fun

- Have confidence in yourself and don't panic

- Pick the right topic for you

- Plan - give yourself time

- Find a supervisor you can work with and be open with

- Relax and enjoy it

- Talk to other students and to your tutors

- Talk to as many people as possible who will listen - if necessary become a bore!

- Be flexible

- Believe your dissertation will work

- Don't lose any sleep

- Learn to type

- It'll all come together in the end

- It's what you learn that matters

- Hand it in and let go!

Towards the end of my journey I came across this poem written by educationalist, Jean McNiff.[7] I have decided to end this 'rough guide' with her poem, because it conveys much that I want to express - about you being the one who knows, or will know, all about doing a dissertation.

> Welcome, my friend, to the land of tomorrow.
> Look for the answers within your own mind.
> Drink of the cup of your joy and your sorrow.
> Seek, and be open to what you might find.
> You, more than I, are aware of your living -
> Yours for the asking, and yours for the giving.
>
> See how you stand on the edge of decision,
> See how you act, and consider, and plan;
> See how your practice is honed to precision,
> See how you weigh what you can't and you can.
> You, more than I, may judge your own ability,
> How to turn chaos to easy stability.
>
> You have the questions to some of my answers,
> I have the questions to some of your own.
> Consciously tuned dialectical dancers,
> We are the knowers of that which is known.
> Yours is the key to your own education.
> Open your mind to the power of creation.

In the Introduction, I wished you 'bon voyage' on your journey. If you are already doing a dissertation, or have decided to take a chance and give it a go, I hope that you will have as much pleasure as I and others have had - also that you succeed in completing your degree and go on to even greater things. Thank you for your company - my journey wouldn't have been the same without you.

# Notes on Contributors

A total of **59 students** contributed directly to this book by completing an open-ended questionnaire, and, more indirectly, by sharing their experiences through informal conversations.

Of the **51 undergraduates**, most had studied at Lancaster University and just over half describe themselves as 'mature students'. Some had gained a high grade for their final-year dissertation whereas others had completed a dissertation in the second year of their degree. 'Novice' undergraduates also shared their accounts of the struggles they were experiencing whilst actually in the process of doing a dissertation. A few contributors, studying at other institutions, were participants of a 'Summer University' course on dissertation-writing held at Lancaster University.

**Eight postgraduates** writing MA dissertations completed a questionnaire and four were also interviewed. Despite the more advanced level of their studies, most of them had no previous experience of doing a dissertation.

**The range of contributors' subject areas and disciplines** include Accounting, Economics, Educational Research, English, Environmental Science, Geography, Health Studies, History, Human Communication, Independent Studies, Linguistics, Management Learning, Operational Research, Psychology, Religious Studies, Sociology and Women's Studies.

# References

Quotation (before title page) Boud, D in Boud, D & Griffin, V (eds) (1987) Appreciating Adults Learning: From the Learners' Perspective London: Kogan Page

## Footnotes

1 Extracts from the poem ITHAKA, by Cavafy, C P (translation by Keeley, E & Sherrard, P) taken from Savidis, G (1975) *Collected Poems* London: The Hogarth Press

2 Williams, P in Foreword to Partington, P (ed) (1993) *Student Feedback - Context, Issues and Practice* Sheffield: CVCP/ USDTU

3 Swales, J (1990) *Genre Analysis* Cambridge: Cambridge University Press

4 Adderley, K et al (1975) *Project Methods in Higher Education*: SRHE Ltd

5 *(ibid)*

6 Williams, M & Horobin, R (1992) *Active Learning in Fieldwork and Project Work* Sheffield: CVCP/USDTU

7 McNiff, J (1993) *Teaching as Learning: An Action Research Approach* London: Routledge